Contents

ALAMY/GETTY

● All transcriptions by Joshua Morris

tes

Essential INTELLIGENCE *for the* EDUCATION PROFESSIONAL

A *Tes* magazine subscription is all you need to stay up to date with the latest education ideas, innovation and insight, plus classroom tips and techniques.

Subscribe today:

Print and Digital package starts from only £30 per quarter.

Digital Only prices start at just £15 per quarter.

Order now: **tes.com/store/magazine**

Kick-starting the conversation on education-related research

How much of what you do in the classroom would you say was evidence based? By that, I mean is the way you teach – or what you teach – backed by reliable studies from the world of academic research?

A decade ago, such a question would have been asked of teachers rarely, if at all. The profession was still largely one of dark arts and intuition, with expertise handed down from generation to generation. Teachers could feel in their gut and see from the results whether something was working.

But then, as Dylan Wiliam explains in chapter one of this guide, the researchers worked out that they needed to be better at communicating what they were doing. They had to be more aware about the potential impact of their research in the classroom, regardless of whether or not they considered it related to education.

As the research became more accessible and moves towards evidence-based practice in other fields, such as medicine, were popularised, interest from teachers grew. Grassroots movements sprang up enabling academics and teachers to converse, the prominence of tools such as the Education Endowment Foundation Toolkit rose and research literacy increased.

Not everyone has embraced the move towards evidence-based practice, however.

Be it due to workload issues, accessibility, time, or a suspicion that the missives from the academic world are not as robust or applicable as they seem, some teachers are keener to trawl through studies than others.

The conversations all this prompts are undoubtedly healthy for the profession. Debate – professional, well-informed debate, at least – is how we progress.

At *Tes*, we wanted to help those conversations to happen: we already had a weekly interview with an academic about their research (*Tes* Talks To), and leading academics writing for us regularly (some of whom are in this guide), and then, in September 2017, we launched our Podagogy podcast.

The idea behind the podcast was to enable academics to speak directly to teachers, forcing them to communicate clearly about the practical applications of their work and its limitations. The success of the podcasts took us by surprise: we get thousands of listeners every week, with some excellent engagement from teachers. The natural next step was to make these interviews even more accessible by putting them in written form.

This guide is the result: the first seven podcasts, edited and with follow-up reading suggestions. We hope they spark some interesting conversations in your school.

Jon Severs, Tes *commissioning editor*

'The idea behind the podcast was to enable academics to speak directly to teachers'

Chapter one

Professor Dylan Wiliam
on applying research
in the classroom

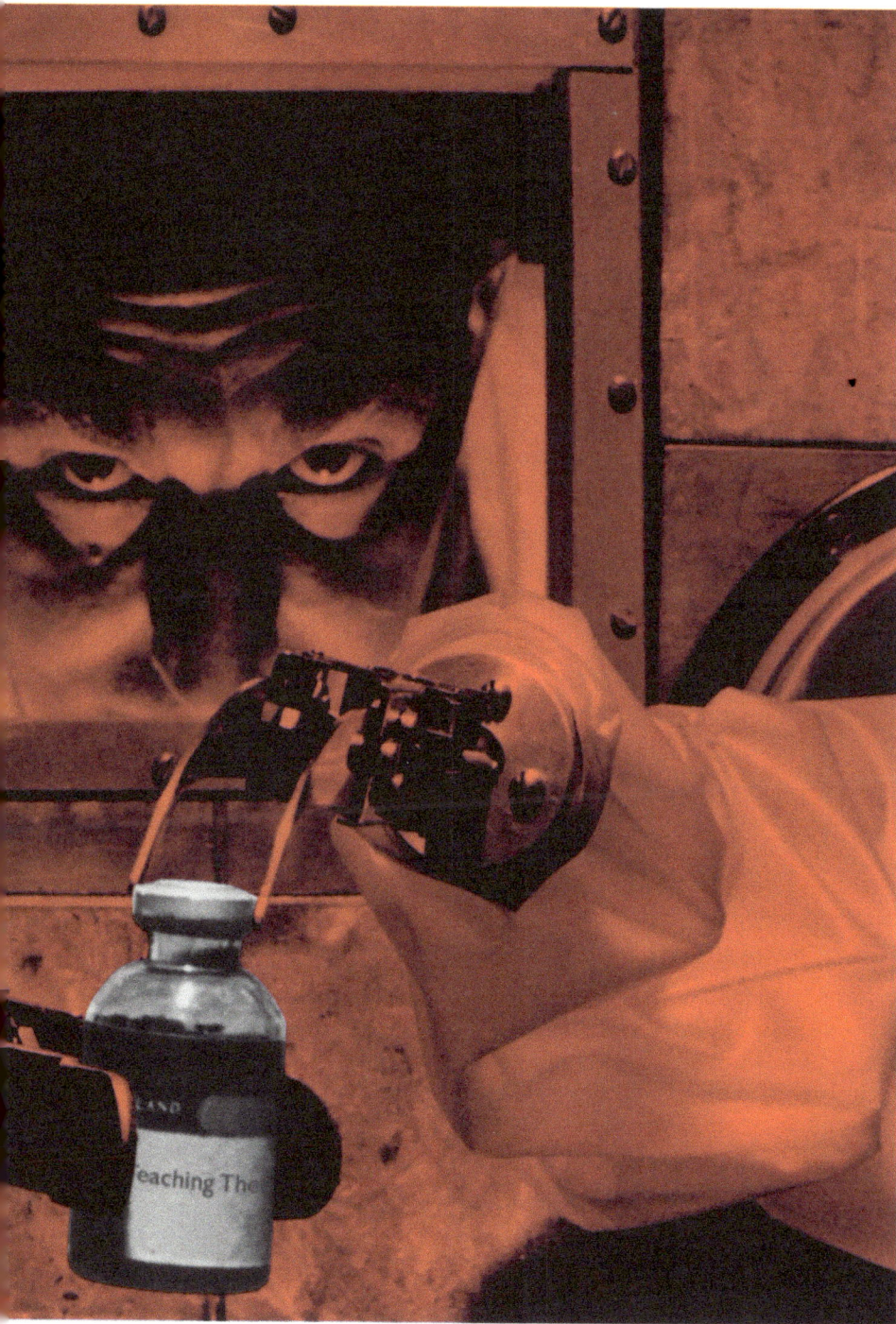

Dylan Wiliam, emeritus professor of educational assessment at the UCL Institute of Education, is renowned for his work on formative assessment and is now a familiar figure within the movement to make teaching a more research-informed profession. In this interview, he talks about the usefulness of the research that is out there and the ways in which teachers are currently consuming it.

How much of a change do you think there has been in the past four or five years in terms of the amount of research that has come into the classroom practice of everyday teachers?
It's been a dramatic change and a very welcome one. Too many teachers in the past found that research wasn't helpful to them, partly because researchers weren't sharing their research in a way that was accessible to teachers but also because a lot of the research that was being done was not particularly relevant to them.

Researchers are now thinking much more about how to communicate their findings to practitioners and we're beginning to get insights into learning that have profound implications for really practical things.

Some of the research is directly related to education and some I've seen used in schools has come from research in different areas. Is there a lot of the latter going on and is that useful and healthy?
Education has always borrowed insights from other fields, partly because I don't think that it makes sense to think of education as a discipline – it's a field of study and it draws on different disciplines.

I think education works well when it draws on sociology, psychology and other fields that aren't directly connected. The danger is that it often goes too far.

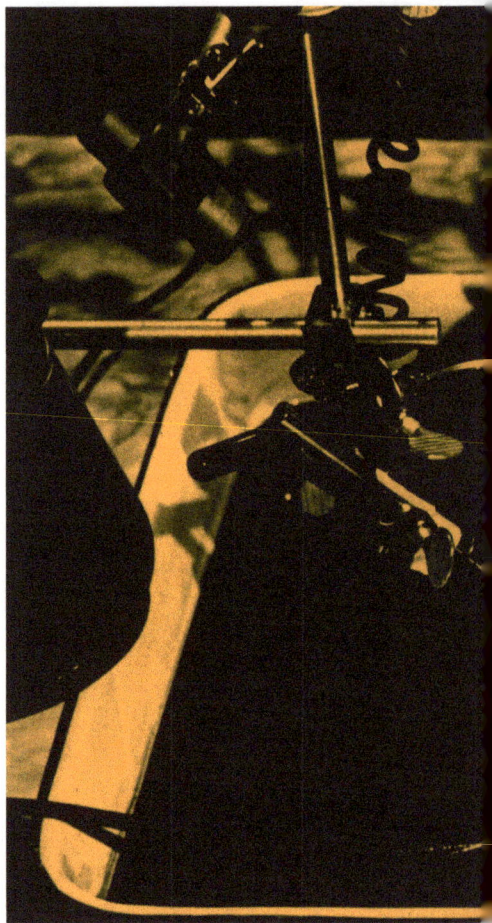

We're always looking for the next big thing in education, so we latch on to ideas and we try to apply them, and often it doesn't work [in schools] because the timescales are wrong.

As the academic Paul Kirschner and his colleagues have pointed out, learning is a change in long-term memory.

If nothing has been changed in long-term memory, nothing has been learned, therefore you can't really evaluate education in

less than six months. You can't tell whether it's a good lesson unless students are remembering what they've been taught months later.

That's why a lot of these things are really hard to apply. So, we often rush to apply insights in rather shallow ways but, on the other hand, I think it's better that teachers are inquiring in new ways and trying to keep up with the latest thinking.

We just need to be a bit more sceptical about how relevant these things are to our practice as teachers.

Could you elaborate on what that scepticism should look like?

Yes, I have often said that what is interesting is not what works in education but under what circumstances does it work?

Take a classic case like class-size reduction. There are some people who say that class-size reduction does work and others who say it doesn't. That's not very helpful. What we need to understand is when does it work?

So, for example, when you reduce class size, you will need more teachers. If you reduce class size from 30 down to 20, for a group of 60 children you used to need two teachers and now you need three. So, you've increased the number of teachers you need by 50 per cent.

The crucial thing then is: are the teachers you're giving new jobs to as good as the teachers you already had? That depends on local employment markets. In one place, class size reduction might work because you're able to bring in really good teachers, but in another place, it might not work because there aren't any available teachers that are any good and you're bringing in people who are a lot less effective. So, researchers deserve some of the blame here because they haven't taken sufficient account of those contextual variables.

However, teachers have been quick to take this and say, "well, anything that a researcher comes up with won't work in my classroom". It's difficult, but I think there's a more profound issue here, which is that working out what a piece of research means for a teacher's practice is more than a simple case of putting research findings into effect. When teachers take on research, they are taking on the task of creating new knowledge, albeit of a distinct and local kind.

The big mistake we've made as teachers and researchers is to underestimate the creativity and the complexity involved in applying research findings to something as complex as teaching.

Carol Dweck has been the biggest victim of that. She's been very transparent in admitting the problems with the application of her research

The thing that people miss about Dweck's work is that, when she talks about growth and fixed mindsets, she's talking about

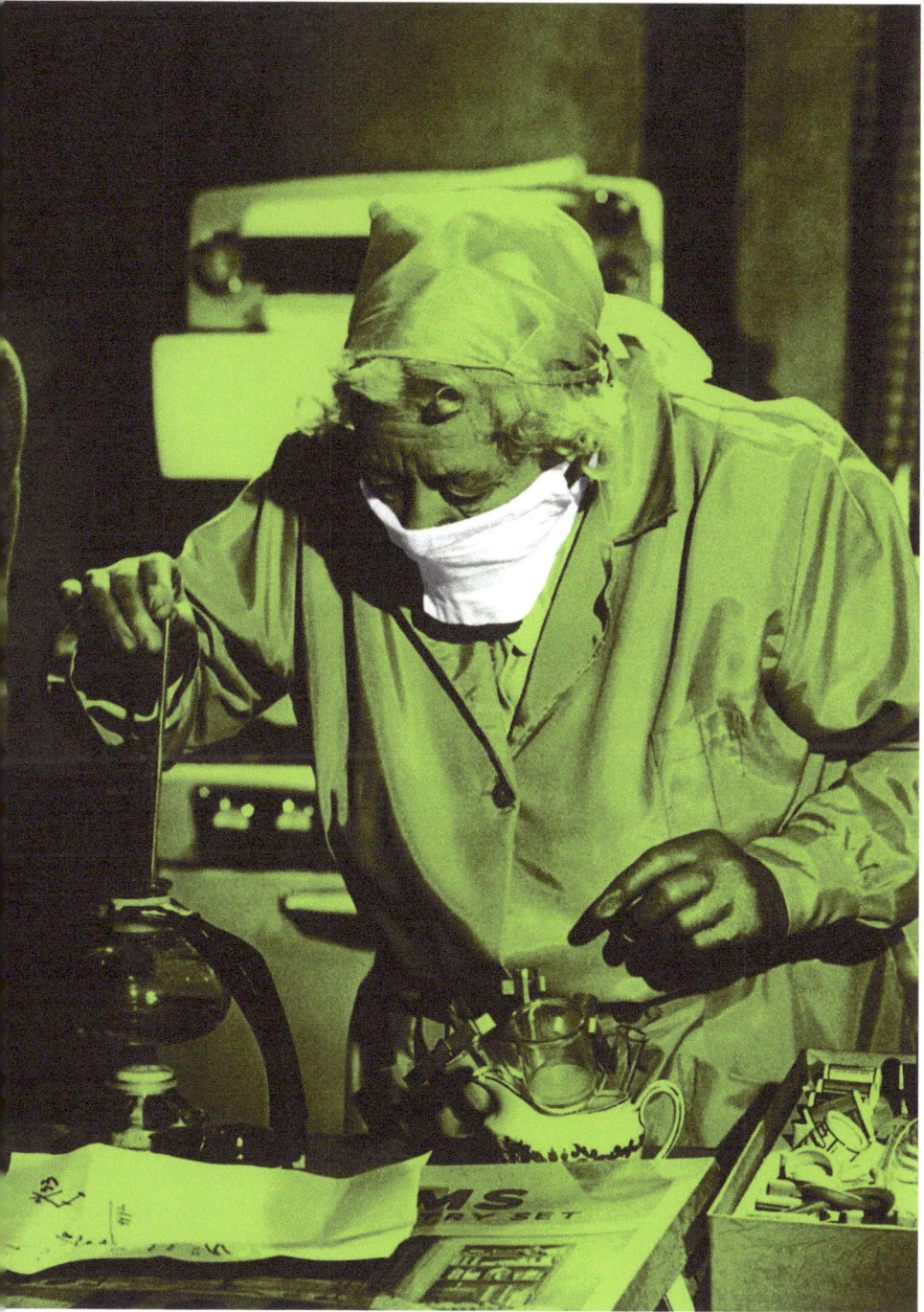

something very specific, which is the way that students view intelligence.

While Dweck's work has been misrepresented, the good news is that it's not particularly harmful. Although the evidence is that it is very hard to change mindset as Dweck defines it – and her work has not been replicated, and the effects on student achievement of mindset interventions were not significant on the conventional levels that we would choose in psychology – the fact that students say, "I can't do this" and the teacher says "yet", then that's very powerful.

What we can do is say, yes, talent exists – some people find this stuff easier than others – but there's no limit to what you can achieve if you work hard at this.

That's the important message for students. Many of the mindset interventions I see happening in schools are along that line of argument and I think that's very healthy.

I know that you're keen on the work of John Sweller. He has attracted some controversy because he discounts large swathes of what has become accepted teaching practice. What should we take from his work (see further reading box, page 14)?

John Sweller is controversial only if you don't want to take any account of the evidence about how human brains actually work. The most important contribution Sweller has made is to point out that one of the ways in which learning can fail to happen when you might think it would is because students become overloaded.

This is based on some incredibly solid science; there is no serious psychologist who disputes the idea that one of the most powerful models for thinking about the way that our brains work is to think about long-term memory and short-term memory. Short-term memory is limited in capacity and duration, and it can't really be increased very much, and therefore the only way to make students smarter is to increase the contents of long-term memory. While it may be controversial, I have no doubt that Sweller is actually fundamentally correct.

The notion of correctness is interesting in research for reasons we have mentioned above

Well, if you take ability grouping in mathematics, the consensus is that grouping

students by ability actually lowers average achievement. It tends to produce losses for the lowest achievers at the expense of gains for the highest achievers, and the losses for the lowest achievers tend to be greater than the gains for the highest achiever producing average achievement.

But, first of all, it may be a value issue. We may think that the small loss for the lowest achievers is more than compensated for by a smaller gain for the highest achievers. Who do you think is the most important? That's a value issue that researchers can't tell you about.

I happen to think that the lower achievers are more important, but that's because I believe in all people being able to participate in a democratic society.

If you had a utilitarian function, it may be that increasing achievement of the highest achievers may produce more economic value – that's something that research can never answer.

But the more interesting issue is the experiments that we've got are the experiments that happen to have been done. So, almost all the educational research that has been done on grouping by ability has just

Dylan Wiliam *is emeritus professor of educational assessment at University College London. In a varied career, he has taught in inner-city schools, directed a large-scale testing programme, served a number of roles in university administration, including dean of a school of education, and pursued a research programme focused on supporting teachers to develop their use of assessment in support of learning.*

reproduced the school setting. In other words, we happen to have, by chance in most schools, the top sets being taught by the best teachers.

Now, it turns out that we know from the work of Simon Burgess, a professor of economics at the University of Bristol, that, actually, the best teachers are more effective for the lowest achievers. You can't conclude that grouping by ability doesn't work if all of the research that has been done doesn't take into account the key variables. So, that's why it's very dangerous to conclude that the research is "this" because we might not have done the right research yet.

So where are we on our education research journey? Are we approaching maturity in terms of the research and how we consume it?

We are making progress but the incentives in the system aren't right yet. There's no doubt that doing research in applied settings with messy real situations is much more difficult than it is doing it in a laboratory. Therefore, it's not surprising that academics who are promoted on the basis of their publications often choose to do research that is easy to do well.

When you do research in real settings, you often end up with findings that are currently inconclusive. So, right now, universities – the way that they incentivise academics to do the work that they do – are driving researchers away from the kind of research that needs to get done.

I want to be absolutely clear: some researchers nevertheless choose to do the best kind of research and the results harm their careers. Right now, the incentives aren't there for academics in education departments to do the research that I think would be most helpful to teachers.

This an edited transcript of a recorded interview that was published in September 2017. You can listen to the full interview here: bit.ly/WiliamonResearch

FURTHER READING

- Dylan Wiliam on the importance of planning the curriculum around how memory works: bit.ly/MemoriesMade
- Dylan Wiliam on nine things every new teacher should know: bit.ly/WiliamNineThings
- John Sweller on cognitive load theory: bit.ly/TesTalksSweller

Chapter two

Professors Robert & Elizabeth Bjork
on how memory works

ALAMY

Robert and Elizabeth Bjork are renowned throughout the world for their research on memory. Together, they run the Bjork Learning and Forgetting Laboratory at the University of California, Los Angeles, and their work on desirable difficulties and retrieval practice has transformed classrooms across the globe. Here, they explain how to match teaching to what we know about how memory works and why group work, and linking learning to a student's interests, is key.

You've spent the majority of your career looking at memory. How certain are we now of how memory works? Do we know for sure how the short-term and long-term memory processes work or are we still dealing in guesswork in some areas?

RB: There's a great deal of research trying to figure things out in more detail. But, in terms of the basic architecture of how people learn and remember, we know a lot more than we did several decades ago.

The architecture of how people learn and remember is very different from the sort of architecture of any standard recording device in almost every way you can think of. [Assuming that our brains work] like some kind of recording apparatus will lead you to do a lot of non-productive things.

EB: Our understanding of memory has come a long way in the past 20 or 30 years, but people still hold on to a lot of misconceptions, so that side of things is definitely still in need of a lot of work. To constantly hear, even in highly educated people, about muscle memory and concepts of that sort, such as "visual learners" versus "auditory learners" and so forth... Those misconceptions out there still need to be worked on.

You talk a lot about "desirable difficulties" in your research – that people need to work hard to remember and that makes the memory easier to recall in the future. And you advise using retrieval practice – returning to information once you have left enough time to "forget" it, quizzing without looking at your notes, revisiting information in different contexts and ways. Do teachers need to be careful with this concept in terms of setting the level of challenge for their students at a point that aids memory?

EB: You've touched on two really important things. It is only desirable if it presents difficulties to the student that, although challenging, they can overcome with effort. But, if it's just totally impossible, then it's not going to be a desirable difficulty; it becomes an undesirable one.

So, there is some sort of tempering that you have to do, depending on certain ages or individuals that you might be teaching. Just like with a video game, you wouldn't throw a player who has just started into level 4 – you would start at level 1, and say, "OK, if you quickly master that one, move on to level 2", and so forth.

The other thing is that, unfortunately, there's a widespread belief, certainly among instructors and learners, that learning should be fun and if it's not fun and seemingly easy then it's not your sort of thing and you should find something else to spend your time on.

That's so embedded that when you're faced with something that is a little bit confusing right now, instead of thinking this is an opportunity for me to learn something I haven't understood before, you think of it

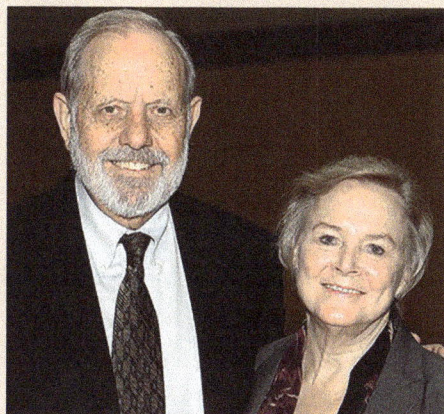

a joint recipient of the James McKeen Cattell Fellow Award, presented by the Association for Psychological Science in recognition of a lifetime of outstanding contributions in research addressing a critical problem in society at large.

Robert Bjork is distinguished research professor in the department of psychology at UCLA. He has served as editor of Memory & Cognition and Psychological Review, co-editor of Psychological Science in the Public Interest, chair of the National Research Council Committee on Techniques for the Enhancement of Human Performance, and chair of the UCLA department of psychology.

He is a recipient of the Society of Experimental Psychologists' Norman Anderson Lifetime Achievement Award and, together with Elizabeth Bjork, the James McKeen Cattell Award from the Association for Psychological Science.

He is a fellow of the American Academy of Arts and Sciences, and was selected to give the 120th faculty research lecture at UCLA in February 2016.

Elizabeth Bjork is professor of psychology and senior vice-chair in the psychology department at the University of California, Los Angeles (UCLA), where she has also chaired the academic senate and received the institution's distinguished teaching award.

She is an elected member of the Society of Experimental Psychologists, a fellow of the Association for Psychological Science, and has served on editorial boards and review panels for the National Institute of Mental Health. Recently, with Robert Bjork, she is

as "oh, this is hard, it must not be for me", or you blame the instructor – you think they are not teaching you correctly because they are making this challenging as opposed to fun and easy.

So, why does that desirable difficulty embed itself in memory easier than something that is easy or fun?

RB: It's not working harder per se as much as it is contending with difficulties [through retrieval practice], and having to think back and relate it to something else. If you can get someone to retrieve something or generate it rather than just present it to them, that's a powerful effect on learning in the long term.

When it comes to spacing content, is there a set time that is optimal or does it differ with each student? Do some need more interleaving (mixing up topics rather than teaching content in discrete blocks) than others?

EB: For some students, it can be longer and they still are able to retrieve back to what you were talking about before and see how it relates. For others, it may have to be a smaller gap and you may have to go over it in more detail.

RB: We can also say that, even if you don't get things perfect for every student, introducing some gap before you come back to information again is going to be better for all students than what we call "mass inner blocking".

For example, research is very clear that if you're a teacher, you can't cover something and find out your students passed the test and then be done with it and assume it's there forever.

Things that are really important need to be revisited later in the class and so much the better if they're revisited in a different context. It's that sort of spacing and revisiting a variation of stuff that will lead to really strong knowledge formation that will remain accessible over time.

EB: A powerful tool that the instructor has is giving a lot of these sort of low-level practice tests – exercises where students have to retrieve things and the teacher can pretty quickly see "OK, a set of students aren't quite ready to move on and I have another set who are ready to move on to something else".

Then they can do some review with that group that is still struggling a little bit until they can retrieve that information at a longer interval.

More testing is an interesting proposition for English teachers, many of whom have been quite vocal against it

RB: Recently, in our lab, we've been looking at all aspects of testing as a pedagogical technique and there are a lot of things to say about it. One is that a major virtue of testing is that it triggers retrieval processes and that can be more important than any free study opportunity would be.

Also, there are multiple other benefits. One is that tests help us to identify what people do and don't understand much more simply than just letting them look at the material again. It has that metacognitive benefit that's telling them where to go

and what they need. The other thing we found in actual classes is, if you introduce lots of low-stakes – and sometimes no-stakes – quizzing at the start or the end of the class, students are very positive about them – they don't feel like they're being assessed.

They feel like it's enabling the learning process, which it really is.

And recently, work by Elizabeth and a couple of graduate students has found that "pre-tests" have great value even when students can't answer any of the questions.

You ask them questions about material that hasn't been covered yet and they will get virtually none of the correct answers. But then that turns out to facilitate their learning when they do get that material.

So, that's something we've been exploring just recently.

That's fascinating. So, say you had a new topic you wanted to study – the Romans – and you did a low-stakes test at the start of that syllabus of work and the students got no answers right, that's still productive in terms of their long-term learning in that topic area?

EB: Correct, and we're still looking at all of the situations in which this would apply. So far, we definitely know it applies in a classroom as well as a lab.

The pre-tests need to be constructed correctly in a way that will get the student to think about what the right answer to this could possibly be. Why it then potentiates their learning is actually a little unclear; we're struggling with that.

One thing is that it probably makes them more interested in the material – just the fact that they weren't quite sure what the answer to the question was.

So, when the teacher gets to that part of the lecture or that part of the lesson, or they're reading about it, they maybe pay more attention because they think back to how they tried to answer the question.

You also talk a lot about the importance for memory of building on previous knowledge?

RB: All new learning builds on old learning. So, past some early point in life, all new learning is a matter of linking it up and relating it to what you already know.

If you're a teacher, your kids are going to come in with very different backgrounds in terms of what they already know and don't know in the field that you're teaching – and that can be an important guide for

how to individualise learning. One way to look at it is as if all the prior learning you have done is potential for new learning.

It sounds like the teacher has to know every student very well to have a good understanding of their background knowledge and then the ability to differentiate a lesson for those different starting points.
RB: That's a really important point. Even at the college level, one thing that characterises gifted teachers is if they can remember back themselves, or understand what things the students they are teaching are interested in and what background they have.

They can make some new material related to that. That can be difficult – how do I link up this material and make it seem relevant, make it seem important, make it seem understandable?
EB: That's one of the very important roles of graduate students who serve as teaching assistants in higher education.

They're much more in tune with the current culture and life of the undergraduate students and so they can help us to understand what we should be relating these things to if we want our students to learn: the things that are important to them outside the classroom in their life. Those people can be a great source of information; they know what it is that the kids care about now, and this culture, and how can I relate this better to the other things they're doing outside of the classroom?
RB: If you can draw an analogy between something now and something they already know, or sometimes even a metaphor – this thing you're trying to learn is like this thing in another domain – those connections are very powerful, partly

because of the very way that our knowledge is stored and linked.

What would be your key take-home message for teachers on memory?
RB: Unless things keep being accessed, they will become inaccessible. It's a fundamental facet of human memory that we're incredibly vast in terms of storage capacity but in terms of what is retrievable, that's a small fraction of that and that can depend on current queues in context.

If we knew you in detail, for example, we could start asking you questions about great friends you had in schooling or in other activities, and many of those names you would not be able to recall.

We could demonstrate easily that those names exist in your memory but, basically, the way human memory works is that we need to be able to recall what's current and relevant, and the fact that things we're not using become inaccessible actually helps us to recall the most relevant information right now.

This an edited transcript of a recorded interview that was published in October 2017. You can listen to the full interview here: bit.ly/BjorksonMemory

FURTHER READING
- A *Tes* article on how memory works, featuring the work of the Bjorks: bit.ly/TruthaboutMemory
- An English teacher, on how she incorporates interleaving into her planning: bit.ly/PlanningandInterleaving
- A cognitive scientist on spaced practice: bit.ly/SpacedScientist

Professor Margaret Snowling
on dyslexia

Professor Margaret Snowling, president of St John's College Oxford, is one of the world's leading dyslexia researchers. Here, she addresses numerous myths about the condition and explains that education is still missing opportunities to help support students with dyslexia at an earlier stage.

There seem to be so many different definitions and assumptions about what dyslexia is. What do you think of when you talk about the condition?
Dyslexia is a difficulty in learning to read and write, specifically in learning to read fluently, and I think you're right that the term has broadened out as it's been used over time but, essentially, it's a problem with learning to read and to spell.

That seems quite broad. Is it easy to identify in children? Does the broad definition give credence to those who say it does not exist?
In recent years, we have been following a cohort of children who are at family risk of dyslexia. So, they have a parent who is affected and we compare them with kids from families where there is no history of reading problems.

If you follow those kids from about the age of three and a half until they are about age eight, and you decide who is dyslexic and who is not, and you look back, you see what characterised the children that went on to be dyslexic. What you see very early on, before reading instruction, is that these children have difficulties with what we call phonological skills – the speech-processing aspects of language. They have difficulty with phonological memory, so they have problems in saying new words. They often have some speech difficulties, and these

can exist without any language problem. Those problems translate into problems with learning letters, where you have to learn to associate the sound with the letter. They translate into problems with phonological awareness, where you have to identify where the sounds are in spoken words. Together, those two things are enough to impact decoding.

I believe in dyslexia because it occurs very early on, before people start arguing about whether it's an effect of the school system, or laziness or lack of parental support.

But there are a lot of complicating factors because dyslexia is a neurodevelopmental disorder, so it's heritable. And the point of neurodevelopmental disorders is that they're highly associated with one another. So, if you're dyslexic, you may also have, for instance, developmental language disorder or attention deficit hyperactivity disorder (ADHD).

If you take ADHD, one of its defining features is that these children have difficulties in organisation, in working memory and in planning. Many people think that's a symptom of dyslexia but it's not. It's just that many kids with dyslexia have symptoms of ADHD as well. This is why I think people are uncomfortable with the concept of dyslexia – because some of these other issues that sometimes get involved really belong to other problems.

If you use the reading and spelling measures [to diagnose dyslexia], you will also pick up children who may be at the bottom of the range for other reasons, like lack of schooling, or having English as an additional language (EAL).

If you take the example of children with EAL, they might be slow at learning to read but, actually, they soon pick up and don't have any decoding problems, unlike children

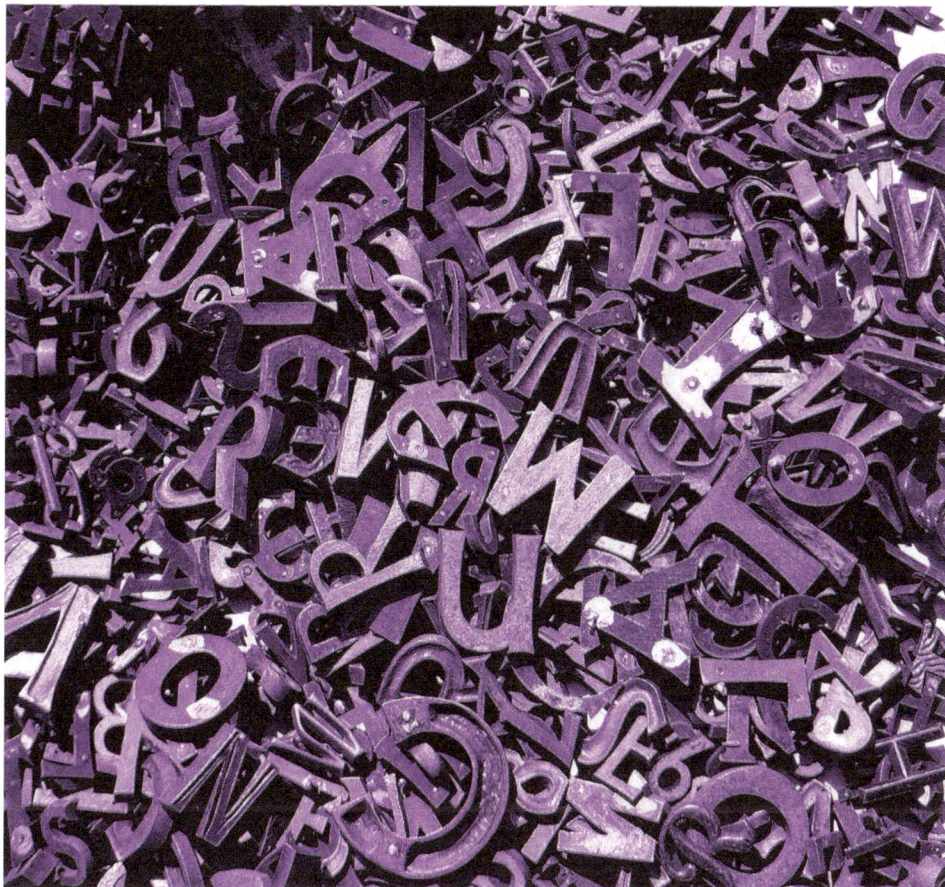

GETTY

with dyslexia. But at one point in time, of course, they might be exactly the same, because they've only just arrived in the country. We have to try to exclude other factors, and we might want to have hypotheses about what the cause is, but still, what we have to do is intervene and monitor.

Have we got the right interventions currently in schools to support dyslexic students?

The best interventions combine training in letter knowledge and phoneme awareness with reading from books. So, as their phonological skills emerge and their understanding of phonics progresses, they need to be practising them in a range of books that are rich in language because, to some extent, their use of language can facilitate or bootstrap the learning.

Like many other neurodevelopmental disorders, the nature of dyslexia does change a bit over time. Initially, it's a reading problem, then it's a problem with spelling, and then it's a problem with reading fluency, so their reading is very slow. Then it can be a problem with writing composition because they're always trailing behind and they're

Margaret Snowling *became president of St John's College, Oxford, in September 2012. Before that, she held a personal chair in the department of psychology at the University of York, where she was co-director of the Centre for Reading and Language. She is a past president of the Society for the Scientific Study of Reading and one of the joint editors of the* Journal of Child Psychology and Psychiatry. *She served as a member of Sir Jim Rose's expert advisory group on provision for dyslexia in 2009 and as an expert member of the Education for All: Fast Track Initiative group in Washington DC in 2011.*

She is a fellow of the British Academy and of the Academy of Medical Sciences. She was appointed CBE for services to science and the understanding of dyslexia in 2016.

not at the point to receive in the classroom what the rest of the class is getting.

The problem comes when you've actually done this intensive work and there's no change – where do you go next? At that point, one really has to start to ask, is this just dyslexia or is there something else as well? Does this child have some kind of language problem? Do they have some kind of attention problem? What else is there?

The other thing to really highlight is their problem with arithmetic, because many children with dyslexia have arithmetic difficulties and this is part of their verbal processing difficulties.

Just as in the way that they have difficulty learning that the sound of "c" is "kuh" and the sound of "h" is "huh", they have some difficulty learning that the number one and the number two go together to make two in a multiplication table, and so on. The nature of what you see [in an individual] at

any time is likely to change. Again, this is one of the reasons that dyslexia can be considered a difficult concept.

You mentioned that signs of dyslexia can be seen very early. Are those signs looked out for in nursery or preschool? It strikes me that's a great place to flag a problem. In your experience, is the training in place at that stage to start the support?

Early on, what I think is critical is that children's language development is monitored, because although early language delay isn't a particularly significant indicator of later language delay, many children who have got early language delay do go on to have dyslexic difficulties.

Generally, if a child has a language delay, it's quite good to tell parents and early-years providers what they might do to facilitate oral language development. At the moment, that's not really being done, and that is a shame. I would say, however, that there is also a group for whom the problems occur later and these are often kids who have compensated very well because maybe they've had a good home literacy environment, maybe they're relying a bit on their good vocabulary to read, and their problems often emerge only a bit later when the amount they have to read increases.

I think academic self-confidence is interesting here since, if you are having difficulty accessing language, this can lead to assumptions about your ability or your potential attainment.

Whenever I used to see kids for assessment of their learning needs, it was always very important not just to say what they needed to do to remediate the problem but also what should be happening to ensure that they keep in sight their strengths and their interests. Because for those doing well in other areas, that can support the difficulties in the reading domain.

Do you think the system is set up in such a way that makes that difficult, though?

It's becoming a bit of a broken record but I think if a child with dyslexia has had really high-quality, evidence-based support for about two years, and they're not really progressing, and they're still struggling, we really have to start thinking about compensation in a big way – that is, we have to start bringing in IT.

There's no reason why children can't use voice-to-text software, planning organisers, dictaphones, but ultimately, it also [comes down to] choice of GCSE subjects and choice of educational options after school.

I do think, in general as a society, we need to have a much better way, or different ways, of going on towards careers, so we have more vocational training and apprenticeships. At the moment, it is a bit like a sausage machine that caters for the average child, or average-to-above-average child, who is going to be able to cope.

With literacy being really important, we need to think of other successful indicators not depending on literacy. We need to have a broader view of what success in school is, because wellbeing is ultimately what we've got to work towards.

For most people, unfortunately, in our society that means being literate. So, how do we foster wellbeing in kids who find literacy problematic?

What would be your main takeaway for teachers on dyslexia, based on the research?

That it is a complex topic and I think that the teacher's role is to monitor the reading and spelling as it develops. [It's important to] have input there to help and also to monitor the child's self-concept and check that they're supporting that as well.

This an edited transcript of a recorded interview that was published in November 2017. You can listen to the full interview here: bit.ly/SnowlingonDyslexia

FURTHER READING

- Why the Comic Sans font does not help dyslexic students: bit.ly/DyslexiaComicSans
- The most common special educational need you have never heard of – developmental language disorder: bit.ly/DevelopmentalLanguageDisorder
- 10 ways to make your classroom dyslexia friendly: bit.ly/DyslexiaFriendlyClassrooms

Chapter four

Professor Carol Dweck
on growth mindset

C arol Dweck, Lewis and Virginia Eaton professor of psychology at Stanford University, is the creator of the highly popular growth mindset theory. The concept has been hotly debated among educators and researchers alike, and has come under intense scrutiny, with highly publicised failed replications of the original research. Dweck does not shun these issues; instead she embraces them, and here she delves head first into the questions behind the theory's validity.

Have you been surprised at the take-up of growth mindset theory in teaching?

The uptake of growth mindset, it's popularity in education, the excitement many teachers are feeling – that is extremely gratifying. At the same time, we've learned so much: we've learned that growth mindset is not as simple a concept as we'd thought. Many people misunderstand it or misuse it. We've really learned in the past couple of years that it's not at all intuitive how to implement it in the classroom.

Where does your definition of growth mindset differ from the definition that is being used in many schools?

Our definition of growth mindset is the idea that talents and abilities can be developed and are not just fixed. They're qualities that can be developed over time through learning, through mentoring, through hard work, through good strategies. And many people have used it that way, but some educators have reduced it to being about effort – they're just telling kids to try harder, "you can do it if you try hard". Far from helping to build a growth mindset, that's called nagging, which has never worked and never will.

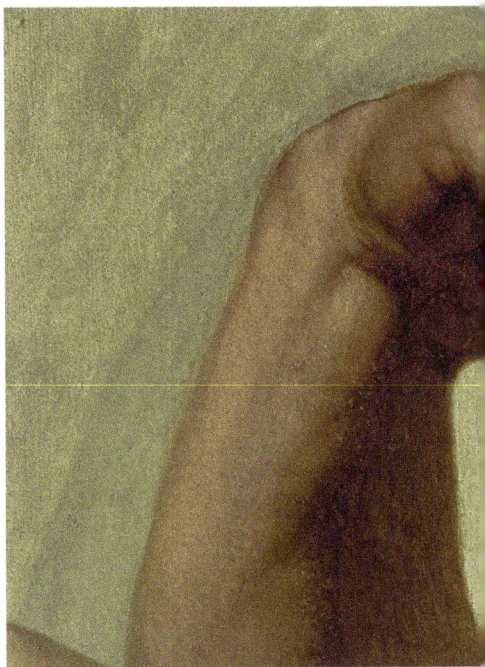

Growth mindset doesn't deny talent or that kids differ from each other. It doesn't say that anyone can be Albert Einstein or Marie Curie. It just says that everyone is capable of growth and, in the end, we have no idea who's capable of blossoming into someone who makes astounding contributions. Some educators think, "I have a growth mindset, I'm open-minded". And that's great, but it's not a growth mindset. Really, it is about the belief that kids are capable of growing their talents and the dedication to making that happen for every student.

Would you say a misunderstanding of the original research – the theory – has been the cause of the failed replications of your work?

Yes, we see some replications that don't really understand the theory. It's got a lot of subtlety.

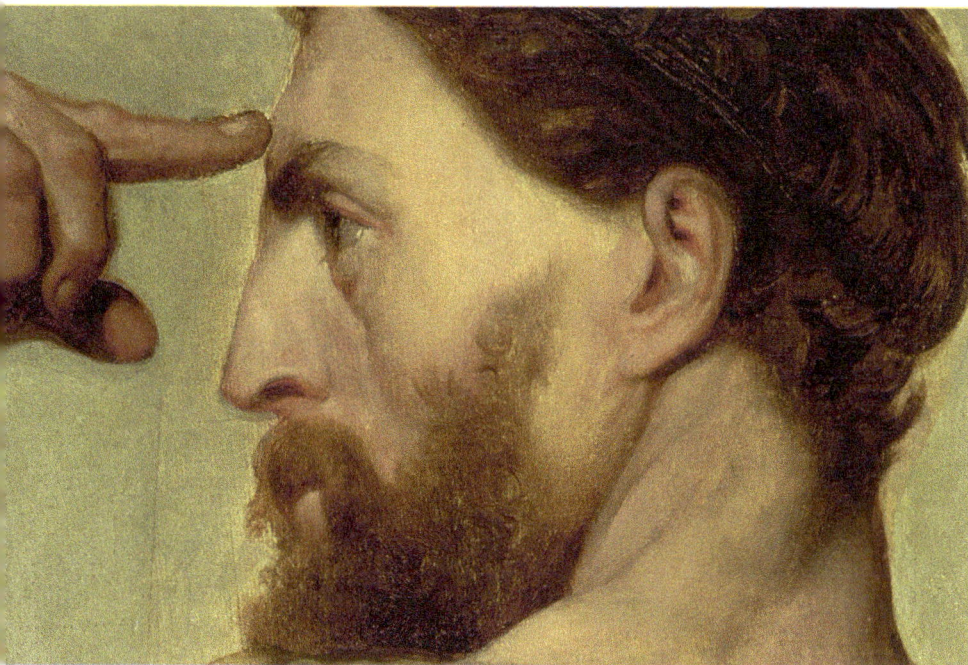

You mentioned you were aware, though, that there have been issues applying the theory in the classroom and I understand you are working on research to help in that?

Once we saw how hard it was to transmit, we said that this is our responsibility. We're not going to say, "educators, you didn't do it right. That may be why you're not reaping benefits. Oh, that's your fault."

We took it as our mission to do research on when the theory translates, when it doesn't, how to do it right, and how to create a curriculum – a step-by-step curriculum – for teachers, so that everybody can do it right.

We don't think it works every time, everywhere. We want to know where it doesn't work and how we can improve it to make it work. So, I feel like we are, in some ways, at the beginning of our journey.

Have you been shocked by the animosity directed at you as a result of some of the failed replications and uses?

We are not putting out a theory that we're saying is the gospel. We're putting out something that says "this is our current understanding". This is the process of science – we're putting it out and we're getting feedback.

And if someone says, "I have a study that says something different", we say, "great! Tell me how I can learn from it".

I think the adversarial relationship is unnecessary. We are eager to learn where we are wrong, where it doesn't work, so that we can make it better.

And I'll never be done with correcting, amending and improving on my work. I don't feel that animosity comes into it. I don't have animosity toward anyone and

Carol Dweck *is one of the world's leading researchers in the field of motivation and is the Lewis and Virginia Eaton professor of psychology at Stanford University.*

Her research has focused on why people succeed and how to foster success. She has held professorships at Columbia and Harvard universities, has lectured all over the world, and has been elected to the American Academy of Arts and Sciences.

Her publication, Self-Theories: Their Role in Motivation, Personality, and Development, *was named Book of the Year by the World Education Federation. Her work has been featured in such publications as* The New Yorker, Time, The New York Times, The Washington Post, *and* The Boston Globe.

I would be concerned if they had any animosity toward me.

In your studies so far, does growth mindset have more of an impact at certain age ranges?

We don't know the answer. Maybe if you are immersed in a really deep, true growth mindset environment early on, you just don't know any other way.

One line of our work shows that you can start detecting a form of mindset in toddlers. It doesn't mean it's stable, it doesn't mean that's rigged for life.

But at around the age of three and a half, children can start thinking they're good or they're bad.

And it might be important at that age, when their conceptions of themselves are forming, to foster this orientation towards growth. But I think the bottom line is, it's never too late.

Your next job is to develop a pedagogy for this, do you have a timescale?

We've only been on the pedagogy job for a few years. It will take many more. It's too soon to say we've got this all wrapped up. But it's not too soon to say we're on the case.

This an edited transcript of a recorded interview that was published in October 2017. You can listen to the full interview here: bit.ly/DweckonGrowthMindset

FURTHER READING

- Analysis by Adi Bloom on the replication issues around Dweck's research: bit.ly/BloomonDweck
- Dweck on why research is not going to give teaching a magic bullet: bit.ly/MagicGrowthMindset
- Dweck on the problems of applying growth mindset: bit.ly/ApplyingGrowthMindset

Chapter five

Dr Sara Baker
on the use of play in education

ALAMY

Sara Baker is principal investigator in the University of Cambridge's Play in Education, Development and Learning Centre. She has been working with teachers, not just to research the role of play in the classroom but also to try to define what play actually looks like. In this wide-ranging interview, she suggests that many of our assumptions are wrong.

When we talk about "play", are we all talking about the same thing – it seems that people have very different ideas about what it actually is?

That's right. Everyone has a different idea about it. There are as many ideas about play as there are different people in the world, I think.

In our centre, we are almost put to the challenge of having to define play. I take the view that it's not really worth doing: there are many different perspectives, there are different types of play, there are different contexts for play, there are different features of a person who is playing or being playful. So, there are lots of meanings of the word and different understandings of it. They're all valuable.

We do have to be quite clear and focused about what we're studying at any one time, though. In my work, we think about play as child-led learning, but there are other people in our centre who study play from a totally different perspective.

For them, it's about play in the context, for example, of a parent and a child playing together. The child could be as young as 12 months. In that case, the type of play will be very different from in a classroom.

Would you class anything regularly done at secondary level as play?

In a secondary school, you might see a

Tes RESEARCH

classroom where students are building a robot, or they're entering a science competition with other schools, or something like that.

That would be very much learner-led learning. So, we might not say child-led anymore, yet it's still learner-led, based on their interests and their own motivations, but with particular learning outcomes that have been thought about in advance.

Some people may be shocked that you would class those things as play...

You can think about playing with words, playing with ideas. Those are forms of play, just as playing video games is. It may not always look like a joyful activity – I've seen people who are very concentrated and take it very seriously – but we would still call that playing.

Do you think that teachers use play enough, then?

It's important to bear in mind that we don't really know when playful learner-led approaches are most beneficial and where the limits of that are.

I'm not going to sit here and say that we all have to adopt playful approaches because it's the best thing in the world, and otherwise we'll never learn anything and everything else is rubbish.

There's more research needed on this because there are a lot of perceptions of the role of play but, without having a research evidence base for when it's most beneficial – and when, actually, another approach is better – we can't really know what the best thing is.

For example, there is evidence that if you want children to learn something specific, taking a learner-led approach is less efficient

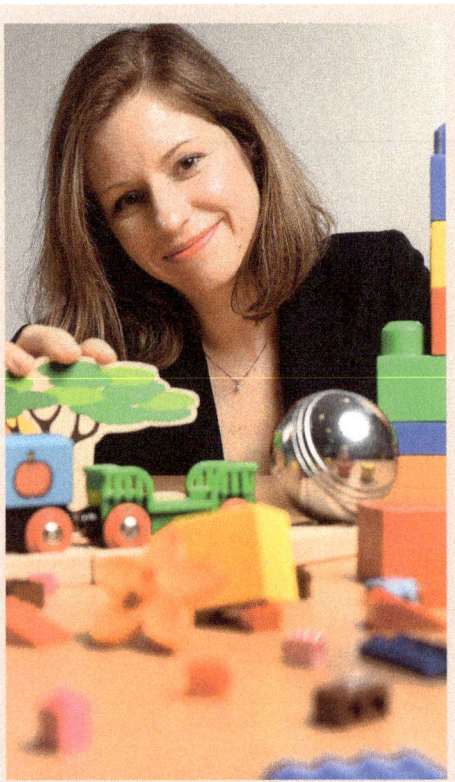

Sara Baker's *research interests are based in cognitive science. She studied for a master's in psychology and cognitive neuroscience at the University of Paris 8 while on placement at the Salpêtrière Hospital's brain imaging unit. She then did a PhD at the Rutgers University Center for Cognitive Science, working with preschool children throughout New Jersey. This led to a three-year Economic and Social Research Council-funded postdoctoral research position within the University of Bristol's Cognitive Development Centre.*

From 2007-10 she was an invited lecturer at the Royal College of Psychiatrists. She held a lectureship in developmental psychology at the University of Salford before joining the University of Cambridge's Faculty of Education in October 2011.

She is currently a principal investigator in the recently established Centre for Research on Play in Education, Development and Learning.

and, perhaps, less effective. They may either take a lot longer to learn it or never get to the particular point you had in mind. So, if it's a very specific goal, maybe it is better to just tell them.

However, as soon as we start to have that conversation, it forces us to think about what our learning objectives are.

If we want them to be very specific pieces of knowledge, fine. If we want to have learning objectives that are more about developing lifelong learners with problem-solving skills and social skills, then we can start to look at other kinds of approaches, and say that maybe they are more effective. There is some evidence that might be the case.

So, can we say anything about the use of play in education with any certainty at the moment?

The field of play research is growing, but there isn't a lot of really solid, consistent evidence that's been replicated in different contexts, so it's a bit patchy.

What I can say is that as soon as teachers start trying to take a more learner-led approach, they realise there are skills that the children need to have in order to engage with that.

For example, kids need to know how to have constructive conversations together. If they can't talk to each other and work in groups for the benefit of everyone, that's going to be a barrier.

That's nothing necessarily to do with the ultimate thing we're trying to do, but it's almost a prerequisite.

It's interesting that play might be getting a bad reputation, mainly because the basics of how you do play aren't in place, so the process is being tarnished by, essentially, the nuts and bolts of getting it right.
Exactly.

The big push for play-based learning is mainly in the Early Years Foundation Stage – would you say that was where it is most suited?
There are huge shifts throughout the pre-school years and right up to the age of about six. Every month, things are changing radically – any parent of a young child has seen that. So, it's true that throughout the Reception year, kids are experiencing a lot of changes in the way they experience the world.

If anything, kids need more structure [at this point]. In terms of the scaffolding that not only parents but also teachers – and even peers – can offer to each other, they're going to need more of that, the less wired up their brains are. So, the more the brain can make sense of the world on its own, perhaps the more playing alongside can happen and the less guidance they should need. That's a big theoretical position, but it's thought-provoking.

Do you think the word "play" stops us having a sensible debate about questions like that?
I don't use the word that much in my day-to-day work because I think it can mean a lot of different things to a lot of different people.

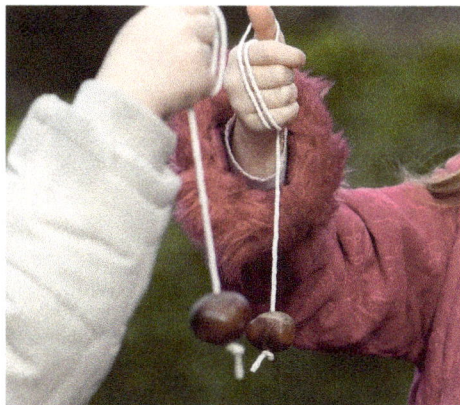

It's a bit like a doctor talking about health. We generally know what it means, but if you want to be specific and you're talking to a patient about something, you're going to talk about the specific thing that they've come to you with. You're not going to talk generally about health all the time because it could be just too vague.

That's why, personally, I think the word "play" is a catch-all. It means a lot of things to everybody but we are trying to make headway on the questions of where the evidence is and what kind of teaching practice we should adopt. It's important to try to be more specific.

This an edited transcript of a recorded interview that was published in October 2017. You can listen to the full interview here: bit.ly/PlaySecondLook

FURTHER READING
- An interview with Sara Baker from *Tes*: bit.ly/BakerTalk
- Using play to teach writing skills: bit.ly/WritingFlourish
- Six steps for successful child-initiated play in EYFS: bit.ly/ChildInitiatedLearning

Chapter six

Professor Daniel Willingham
on how we learn to read

Daniel Willingham, professor of psychology at the University of Virginia and author of books such as *Why Don't Students Like School?* and *The Reading Mind*, is one of the world's leading experts on reading. He talks through the three processes children need to get right to become successful readers and why teachers need to overcome the fact that phonics resources tend to be "boring".

In your book *The Reading Mind* you break down reading into three steps
Yes, I think the three processes of reading that need to be in place for a reader to be successful are first, fluent decoding; second, comprehension; and third, motivation. Each on its own is quite complex.

Could you talk through decoding?
The reason we call it decoding is that print is a code. It's a code for sound. Letters correspond to speech sounds, and so children need to learn how to break that code. Of course, there's an enormous amount of controversy over how that's taught, I think, even more in Britain than in the US.

You're referring to the whole-word versus phonics debate, and all the variations in between. Why do you think phonics is so controversial? Every school does it here in England now, yet its reputation is still that it's something you have to take sides on.
Harvard academic Jeanne Chall wrote a report in the 1960s that was the first really systematic literature review of comparing phonics with other methods, chiefly whole-word teaching, at that time. She concluded that phonics had the edge. Most reports – virtually all – since then have drawn the same conclusion.

But Chall, in that very first report, said there was the potential to go overboard in phonics. You can't simply sit kids down with dull worksheets and drill them in phonics lessons for hours at a time.

That is an over-correction, or a misguided, well-intentioned but terrible method of teaching, and I think that's what people respond to when you look at the materials of phonics instruction – they frequently are pretty boring. Chall also noted that,

through enthusiasm and creativity, teachers can make it more fun for kids.

So, is it the teacher or the phonics that makes the difference?

Chall says that the biggest difference across different reading instruction programmes is the teacher, but if we're looking at programmes, yes, you would definitely go with a phonics programme. That's why it's controversial. When we think about learning to read, one of our great concerns is that children will love reading. You start looking at phonics worksheets and you say, "my gosh, this is not the way to get kids to love reading".

If a child comes to school already having learnt whole words by sight, is the transition to phonics harder?

That's a great question. If there is systematic research on that, I don't know about it. But my guess, and I want to emphasise that this is a guess, is that if you've done a bit of that sort of learning at home, it's probably not going to interfere with phonics learning.

What problems can be encountered at this stage?

When we think about learning to decode, in the early stages, there are three things that have to happen.

Children have to be able to differentiate individual letters. So, they need to be able to see that a lower case "b" is not the same thing as a lower case "d" even though they look similar – the visual aspect.

Then there's the auditory aspect: you need to be able to hear that a "b" and a "d" sound different.

Then there's the matching problem. You need to learn which visual stimulus the letter looks like and then that it goes with a particular sound. It's a process of memory and association.

There is a lot of emphasis, especially among parents, on the third of these, because our language and our spelling system seem so opaque and arbitrary.

But it is pretty clear that among kids who really struggle with reading, it's the second process – the hearing of individual speech sounds – that is more often a problem. So the children who come into school already having some facility with that definitely have an advantage.

There is substantial literature showing that certain types of wordplay that you commonly find in nursery rhymes, for example, are helpful in getting kids to hear individual speech sounds, because when you hear a rhyme, you hear that there is something similar, and that helps you to detect the difference between, say, "bed" and "dead". The only difference between those is the first speech sound. So that helps you hear them individually.

Does whole-word reading have any advantages?

In principle, you could teach kids to read that way but the problem is that it would take an enormous amount of time and an enormous amount of practice. This would really be deadly boring. You're talking about months and months of vocabulary.

OK, so stage two: comprehension

No one thinks all that much about comprehension usually until the middle elementary grades, when children are perhaps 9 or 10 years old.

That's when the expectations for reading comprehension suddenly increase. It's when most of the children in the class become fluent decoders and fluency continues through middle school.

[Before this age] it used to be good enough that they would decode and say the words out loud, but now our expectations increase: "you've got that part, now you need to be able to understand".

That's when many children suddenly reveal that they are having a problem in reading comprehension.

But it's a problem that was there all along?

I don't know if it's called this in Britain, but in the US it's known as the fourth-grade slump.

Children who come from low-income homes, in particular, they're reading at grade level until they are about 9 or 10 years old.

Then, all of a sudden, it's as though they're falling off a table. They're just not

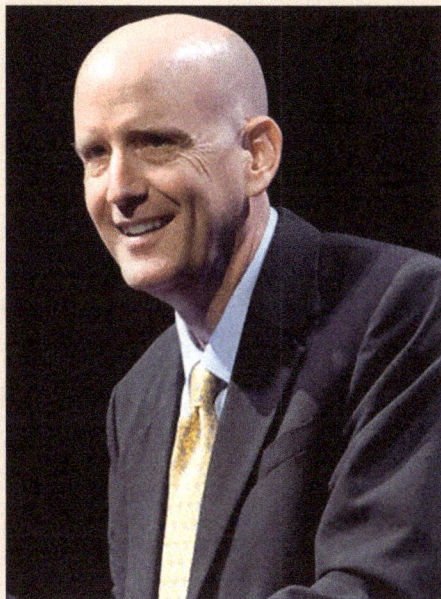

Daniel Willingham *earned his BA from Duke University in 1983 and his PhD in cognitive psychology from Harvard University in 1990. He is currently professor of psychology at the University of Virginia, where he has taught since 1992. Until about 2000, his research focused solely on the brain basis of learning and memory. Today, he is one of the leading voices on reading.*

He writes the "Ask the Cognitive Scientist" column for American Educator *magazine, and is the author of* Why Don't Students Like School?, When Can You Trust the Experts?, Raising Kids Who Read *and* The Reading Mind.

His writing on education has appeared in 15 languages. In 2017, he was appointed by President Obama to serve as a member of the National Board for Education Sciences.

reading as well and this is because the reading tests have changed.

The reading tests used to have low expectations for comprehension and focus mostly on decoding. Now there are suddenly comprehension tasks and the low[-income] kids aren't doing as well.

What's really behind this, and this is actually something else that Chall pointed out (but there has been a lot of work on this since then), is the fact that comprehension is so driven by background knowledge.

If you know something about the topic of the text that you're reading, you have an enormous advantage over someone who doesn't know anything about that topic.

So when we talk about a comprehension deficit in low-income kids, this is mostly a knowledge deficit – not necessarily that they don't know anything, it's just that they don't know the right things.

Are you saying that there's a lack of knowledge in low-income households or that it might not be the knowledge that you need to access the reading texts they are being tested on?

There is a little bit of controversy over the latter because I would say it's an optimistic and egalitarian view.

We like the idea that it's just that these kids know different things. But the fact is, their environment is not as rich as the environment of the wealthier kids. They don't have the same opportunity that the wealthier kids have.

So it's probably a good guess that they simply don't know as much?

I think you're probably right – they do know some other things the wealthier kids don't, and it's that these things are not the kind of things you need to understand a text of the sort that you will encounter in school.

But I think it also can't be denied that learning opportunities are just reduced for these kids. They're not travelling as much, they're not as exposed to as many ideas and books.

It's a narrower band of knowledge, basically. They might have a good knowledge of less stuff?

That's right. This is not to do with raw ability and whether or not they can learn, it's about what the opportunities have been and the experiences they've had.

When we think about reading comprehension, a lot of times, people think about this as a skill. They think about it as something that we can teach strategies for, and we can do a little bit of that. But the truth is, reading comprehension is really listening comprehension.

Once you're a good decoder, what you're doing when you're reading is the cognitive equivalent of listening to somebody talk.

There is very little difference and so, when you think about it that way, it's like, how much better can I make a child at listening? I can give them strategies to help them stay on task, so that they really are listening. I can give them strategies to make sure they're trying to coordinate meaning of different things that have been said.

These are the kinds of things we tell kids to do in reading comprehension strategy, and that's all appropriate and helps a little bit, but doesn't help that much. Because, ultimately, the real key to comprehension is knowing the vocabulary that's being used and then, crucially, having background knowledge that helps you fill in communication gaps when people write.

That brings us to your third step: motivation

What I would say regarding motivation is that I don't see any reason not to talk to children about different types of reading work and to acknowledge that this is hard.

I think it's appropriate – and may be essential – to tell children that this is difficult work that we're doing here: "I'm asking you to do things with this text, analyse it in ways that you wouldn't do if you were just reading for fun".

And tell them there are different things that we do with text. So, you might say, "right now, we're reading this novel but, nevertheless, we're going to do really difficult things with it. It's a challenging text in the first place, and then I'm going to ask you to do some work with this text that's challenging.

That's not the same as the reading that you would do at home for fun. At home, for fun, you can pick whatever you want. It can be easy: you can pick it up at the ending if you want to, you can skip around, but none of that is really OK when we're doing this type of work – and this type of work, I hope and expect, is going to be satisfying to you."

So – and let me be clear – I don't know of any research indicating that what I've just said is actually going to be effective, but it's the way I can think of that might help children make that distinction.

What we're trying to do is get them to do work that's pretty challenging in school; work that we think is appropriate to help them grow as readers but, at the same time, not end up with them thinking "gosh, reading is awful, it's mentally taxing, it's difficult. I end up reading books I don't really like. I have to slog through it", and so forth. We don't want that to pollute the potentially positive attitude towards leisure reading.

Do you need to make room for pleasure reading in school, too, then?

In *Raising Kids Who Read*, I came out in favour of teachers and schools at least considering doing something like "drop everything and read", exactly because it's about the lowest pressure I can think of that will get kids to do some reading for pleasure. If you are not doing it at home, you've got 20 minutes a few times a week, or whatever it ends up being, where you can read purely for pleasure.

One hopes that you've got a wonderful role model in the teacher who is helping you think through "how do I select a book for pleasure? How do I think about it after I'm done with it?" – all the things that are second nature to leisure readers, probably because they learn them at home.

We do know that leisure reading is associated with positive reading outcomes for kids. If we can kick-start that in schools, it would be wonderful, so even though the research literature on it is thin, I think it's worth the risk.

This an edited transcript of a recorded interview that was published in September 2017. You can listen to the full interview here: bit.ly/WillinghamonPhonics

FURTHER READING

- Professor Kate Nation on shared reading: bit.ly/NationonSharedReading
- Professor Jessie Ricketts on oral vocabulary: bit.ly/RickettsonOralVocab
- Poet Roger McGough on nursery rhymes being literacy powerhouses: bit.ly/McGoughonCockRobin

Chapter seven

Professor Uta Frith
on autism

GETTY

U ta Frith is one of the world's leading experts on autism and emeritus professor of cognitive development at University College London. She began studying autism in 1966 at a time when it was an emerging field of research. She now says we are a much more autism-aware society but that many myths and misunderstandings still remain about the condition, particularly in schools.

You've been researching autism for a very long time – attitudes have shifted significantly, I expect?
Yes, it isn't just me anymore who is so fascinated by autism – it really was in 1966. I did my PhD with autistic children because it seemed, to me, much more fascinating than any other subject I could study. Now, we are a much more autism-aware society.

Do you think that awareness has come with a full picture of autism?
There is certainly a comfortable image of what autism is and that also shapes the way that people with autism present themselves – there is no doubt about this.

At the moment, we are struggling to understand the enormous variety of individual differences [within autism]. It seems to me that, in our now autism-fascinated, autism-aware society, we love to see the extraordinary ones, the most talented ones, the ones who are just amazing in their abilities. We don't really see the other end of the spectrum any more.

People now feel that autism is something that they could really be proud of – you might not fit in so easily to society and groups and so on, but the general popular conception is that you might make up for that with amazing abilities. The truth is that this is only true in exceptional cases. Those at the other extreme live in a world that is incredibly limited and restricted.

Teachers seem fascinated by autism. When we publish advice, it does extremely well. Does that represent a curiosity about the condition or do you think that is a fear about "I have someone I don't know how to help"?
It could well be a mix. I'm really delighted that teachers are interested because, to me,

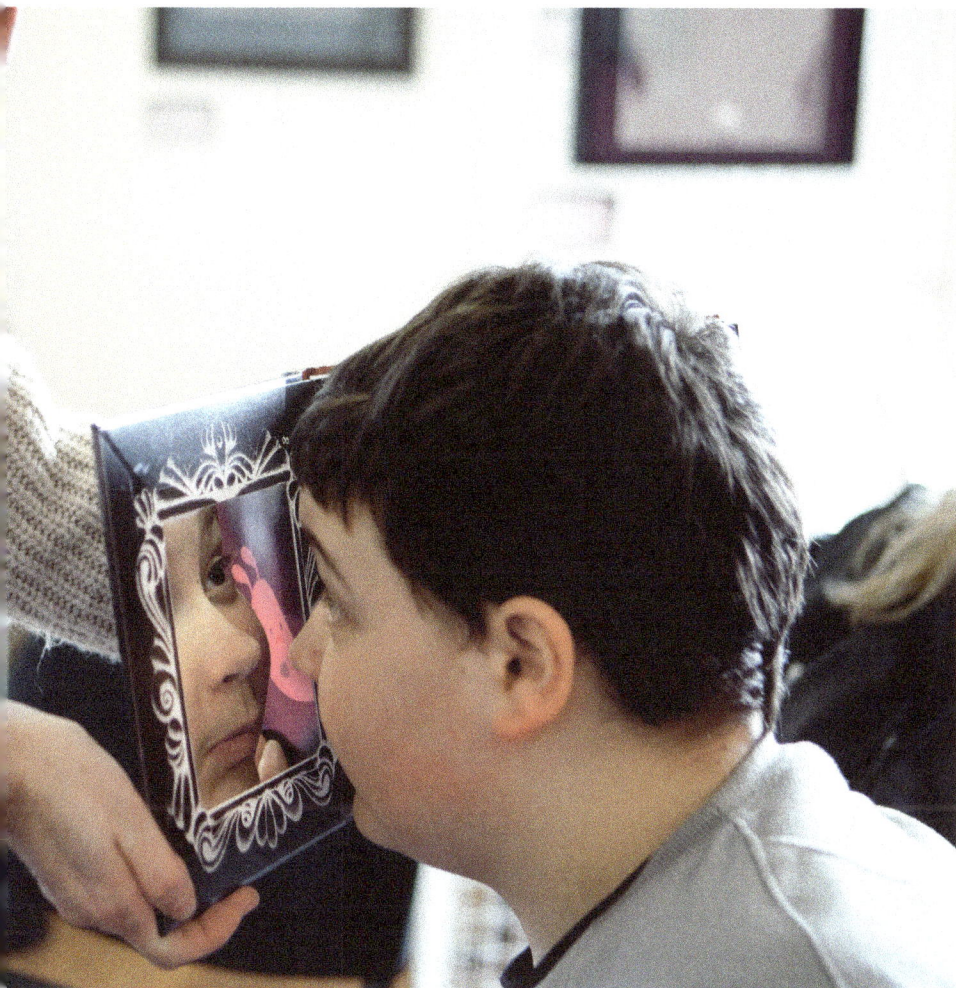

they are the absolutely key people. Education is really the only thing that we can do that helps autistic children of all kinds, with all kinds of difficulties.

But teachers are craving more information, and it's not so easy to get good information. We have this problem with the internet, and social media in general, that so much is presented and you can't quite distinguish what is hype and what we should take seriously.

I'm very interested in having ways of responding to teachers' questions about this. [We should] give them extra training, and really inform them about research that is sound and of high quality.

But I have tremendous respect for teachers who seem to, quite intuitively, find ways to deal with some challenging children.

I think they could also teach the scientists things because they clearly have methods of guiding a child in a very beneficial way.

They can, for example, relax and de-stress, [children] and thereby create motivation to learn.

With autistic children, in the mainstream system at least, there tends to be an assumption that they will be socially reclusive and not like large groups

That's one of the things that needs to be dismantled – it's one of those myths that linger, like the other myths that autistic people don't have empathy – absolutely not true. It may be true for some but it's not a necessary feature at all.

The other thing that people think is that autistic children don't even feel emotions because they don't recognise emotions in others. Again, that's an absolute myth because teachers will tell you, and parents will tell you, that they have very strong emotions.

Is there a sort of phenomenon of "passing" as well – that some autistic children learn to cope and schools may think all is fine but it is not?

I know what you mean. It's very interesting to talk about that. In terms of compensation, this is not trying to improve a very low level of skill bit by bit, it's actually doing something different.

There's an interesting paper that recently appeared, by my colleague Francesca Happe and her student Lucy Livingston, and it's all about conceptualising what compensation means in autism.

They've come up with a wonderful distinction between shallow compensation and deep compensation.

Shallow compensation is when you get from your teacher rules on how to behave, what to do, what not to do, in concrete

Uta Frith *is a developmental psychologist with a special interest in autism and dyslexia. She is an advocate for the advancement of women in science and has founded support networks for female scientists. She is also interested in ensuring that neuroscience research remains relevant to education and lifelong learning.*

Frith was made an honorary DBE in 2012 for services to clinical science. She is a fellow of the Royal Society, the British Academy and the Academy of Medical Sciences. She is emeritus professor of cognitive development at University College London and research foundation professor at the faculties of humanities and health sciences, Aarhus University, Denmark.

terms – a wonderful recipe, which enables you to have a very good conversation as an autistic person. As the other person [in the conversation], you would never guess that they're autistic.

But it's shallow compensation because, on another day, at another time, or if you spend a whole day with that person, you will suddenly realise that they can't keep up the huge effort that this thing demands.

With deep compensation, the authors suggest in this paper, you have the possibility of really working out a solution to problems that other people – ordinary people like us – don't have to work on at all.

Do you see any issues with the variety of terms and phrases that are used to describe autism? There seems to be so many options and preferences...it is easy to offend?
I know, it's very tricky and interesting – I'm sure a cultural historian should really

go and look at this because there have been many changes. For example, there was a time where you were really [frowned upon] if you used the terms "autistic individual"or "autistic child" – you would only be OK if you said "a child with autism" or "an individual with autism".

Even with "autism", maybe you should say "autism spectrum", which allows you a huge umbrella of things, or maybe just "spectrum", or maybe just "different". You have that fantastic term "neurodiversity".

That's the one I hear a lot now. It seems to be the term used most commonly
It is a huge attempt, I can really understand it, of saying "we must do our best to remove the stigma, to really help these people to feel part of [everything], to feel welcomed". It is very difficult to uphold this kind of sentiment, though.

There are lots of people who are autistic and are really suffering, their parents are

suffering, and they seem to be invisible. And I think they would be more invisible the more we use words like neurodiversity.

If a teacher knew they were going to have a child with autism in their class, what should their approach be? Would it be to read around the research, or is a lot of that inaccessible? Would it be talking to the parents? Would it be talking to the child themselves? Or all three of those things?

I think this is the problem. There ought to be a kind of training that combines hands-on experience and reading good research [but it does not seem to be out there].

What is your view on the mainstream versus special school debate for children with autism?

The thing about it is that [the right place] might change during a child's life. They might try it in a mainstream school for a year or two and then [it might] not work anymore, and [they find that] special education is far better for them.

Most of the time my respect for a special education setting is absolutely high. I think they are doing such a marvellous job, while in the mainstream maybe there are going to be problems.

For example, there are always these problems of bullying that seem to be very hard to fight against or eradicate. All parents want their children to be protected from that. So that is the kind of consideration.

And some children with special needs, especially those who have these kinds of abnormalities that make them intellectually disabled, will need a very long time to learn. They are slow at learning but they will learn. To put them together with mainstream children doesn't seem effective. I think more time is needed for them.

I agree with this argument – their school time needs to be longer than the school time for other children. They can go on and on learning. In fact, people have argued that lifelong learning is what really goes on in autism.

This an edited transcript of a recorded interview that was published in November 2017. You can listen to the full interview here: bit.ly/UtaFrithonAutism

FURTHER READING

- *Tes* interview with Uta Frith: bit.ly/FrithInterview
- *Tes* Special educational needs and disability columnist Gemma Corby on supporting girls with autism: bit.ly/SupportingGirlsAutism
- Corby addressing some of the key myths around autism: bit.ly/DispellingAustismMyths

Tes have partnered with SMART to help inspire greatness in every child

For these articles and more visit the hub:
www.tes.com/inspiregreatness

- If we want pupils to excel, we must cherish our teachers and here's how

- Greatness isn't what pupils do, it's what they are

- How can teachers inspire greatness in children

- Children can change the world - we just need to listen

- SMART is signing the You Matter manifesto - and you can too

The SMART hub:
www.tes.com/inspiregreatness

SMART. ❀tes

Lightning Source UK Ltd.
Milton Keynes UK
UKHW021831280219
338217UK00009B/479/P

9 780995 741553